D1161070

WHAT IF ELEPHANTS DISAPPEARED?

By Theresa Emminizer

Gareth Stevens
PUBLISHING

Please visit our website, www.garethstevens.com. For a free color catalog of all our high-quality books, call toll free 1-800-542-2595 or fax 1-877-542-2596.

Library of Congress Cataloging-in-Publication Data

Names: Emminizer, Theresa, author.
Title: What if elephants disappeared? / Theresa Emminizer.
Description: New York : Gareth Stevens, [2020] | Series: Life without animals | Includes index.
Identifiers: LCCN 2018058240| ISBN 9781538238103 (paperback) | ISBN 9781538238127 (library bound) | ISBN 9781538238110 (6 pack)
Subjects: LCSH: Elephants–Conservation–Juvenile literature. | Endangered species–Juvenile literature.
Classification: LCC QL737.P98 E48 2020 | DDC 333.95/967–dc23
LC record available at https://lccn.loc.gov/2018058240

Published in 2020 by
Gareth Stevens Publishing
111 East 14th Street, Suite 349
New York, NY 10003

Copyright © 2020 Gareth Stevens Publishing

Designer: Laura Bowen
Editor: Theresa Emminizer

Photo credits: cover, p. 1 mbrand85/Shutterstock.com; pp. 3-24 (series art) De-V/Shutterstock.com; p. 5 Dmytro Gilitukha/Shutterstock.com; p. 7 (African elephant) Four Oaks/Shutterstock.com; p. 7 (Asian elephant) Independent birds/Shutterstock.com; p. 9 Riccardo Livorni/EyeEm/Getty Images; p. 11 Christer Fredriksson/Lonely Planet Images/Getty Images; p. 13 Jez Bennett/Shutterstock.com; p. 15 SouWest Photography/Shutterstock.com; p. 17 Nuamfolio/Shutterstock.com; p. 19 Jami Tarris/Corbis Documentary/Getty Images; p. 21 Claudia Paulussen/Shutterstock.com.

Printed in the United States of America

CPSIA compliance information: Batch #CS19GS: For further information contact Gareth Stevens, New York, New York at 1-800-542-2595.

CONTENTS

Boldface words appear in the glossary.

Mighty Mammals

Elephants are the biggest land animals in the world! The biggest can weigh up to about 14,000 pounds (6,350 kg) and stand up to about 13 feet (3.9 m) tall. Sadly, these gentle giants are in danger. What would happen if they disappeared?

African and Asian Elephants

There are two species, or kinds, of elephants—African and Asian. Asian elephants live in India and Southeast Asia. African elephants live in sub-Saharan, central, and West Africa. African elephants are larger and have tusks. Asian elephants are smaller and only some have tusks.

African elephant

Asian elephant

7

A Keystone Species

Elephants are so big they can change the landscapes they live in. Just by moving and eating, they help keep their **ecosystem** healthy. Elephants are a keystone species. That means other plants and animals in their ecosystem need them to **survive**.

Giant Footprints

As they walk, African elephants leave deep footprints in the earth. These fill with water and become **habitats** where thousands of tiny **creatures**, such as mites and leeches, make their home. Footprint pools allow for high **biodiversity**, which is key to a healthy ecosystem.

11

Helping Plants Grow

Plants **depend** on elephants to survive. Elephants tear down trees, making room for new plants to grow. They also spread seeds. Elephants eat up to 400 pounds (180 kg) of plants a day. As they travel, they leave plant seeds behind in their droppings.

What Will Happen?

Many trees in elephant habitats need elephants to spread seeds. If elephants disappear, these trees could, too. If the trees disappear, the soil won't have roots to hold it in place. Rain will wash the soil into rivers. Too much soil will cause rivers to dry up.

15

What Harms Elephants?

Elephants spend much of their time traveling, looking for the food and water they need to survive. Unfortunately, elephant habitats are shrinking. **Climate change** is drying up habitats, and people have built over much of the land elephants depend on to survive.

Elephants in Trouble

The number of elephants in the world is shrinking. Asian elephants are endangered. That means they are in danger of becoming extinct, or dying out completely. African elephants are vulnerable, which means they are likely to become endangered soon.

How You Can Help

How can you protect elephants? By sharing what you know! When more people know about a problem, they can help fix it. You can also go online. Ask an adult to help you find a website for a wildlife **protection** group.

GLOSSARY

biodiversity: the different kinds of life in an environment shown by numbers of different kinds of plants and animals

climate change: long-term change in Earth's climate, caused partly by human activities such as burning oil and natural gas

creature: an animal-like being

depend: to need something

ecosystem: all the living things in an area

habitat: the place or type of place where a plant or animal naturally lives and grows

protection: keeping something safe

survive: to live through something

FOR MORE INFORMATION

BOOKS

Hurt, Avery. *Elephants*. Washington, DC: National Geographic Society, 2016.

Simon, Seymour. *Elephants*. New York, NY: Harper Collins, 2018.

WEBSITES

Roots & Shoots
www.rootsandshoots.org/
Find out how you can help elephants and other animals.

World Wildlife Fund
www.worldwildlife.org/species/asian-elephant
Learn more about Asian elephants and how they live.

INDEX